ECO-GROUPS

JOINING TOGETHER TO PROTECT THE ENVIRONMENT

John Hamilton

Published by Abdo & Daughters, 4940 Viking Drive Suite 622, Edina, Minnesota 55435.

Library bound edition distributed by Rockbottom Books, Pentagon Tower, P.O. Box 36036, Minneapolis, Minnesota 55435.

Cover Photo by: Vic Orenstein
Inside Photos by: The Bettmann Archive, Peter Arnold, Inc., Dayton Hudson Corp.

Edited By Sue L. Hamilton

LIBRARY OF CONGRESS CATALOGING-IN-PUBLICATION DATA

Hamilton, John, 1959-
    ECO-groups : joining together to protect the environment / written by John Hamilton.
        p. cm. — (Target Earth)
    Includes bibliographical references and index.
    Summary: Provides information about the history and purpose of such environmental groups as the Sierra Club, the Nature Conservancy, Greenplace, and Kids for Saving Earth.

    1. Green movement -- United States -- History -- Juvenile literature. [1. Green movement -- History. 2. Environmental protection -- History. 3. Nature conservation -- History.] I. Title. II. Series.
GH 195.5.H36   1993   363.7'0525'0973--dc20
                                [B]

International Standard Book Number:	Library of Congress Catalog Card Number:
1-56239-210-7	93-7596

 Thanks To The Trees From Which This Recycled Paper Was First Made.

Let's Begin Here.

- Global warming.

- The ozone hole.

- Rainforest destruction.

- Landfills overflowing.

Sometimes saving the Earth can seem like a pretty overwhelming task, especially when you're a kid. Sure, you recycle your trash, you turn out the lights when you leave a room, and you even got your mom and dad to help you plant a tree in the backyard.

But when compared to millions of acres of rainforest getting slashed and burned every year, your efforts can seem pretty insignificant. What's a kid to do? Join an eco-group, that's what! But before you spend your hard-earned money on the first environmental group that comes knocking at your door, you have to find the one that best fits your interests. Some are radical, with members who will literally chain themselves to trees to stop forests from being cut down. Other groups think a conservative approach is more constructive. These groups try to win environmental battles by passing tough laws against polluters.

Last year more than 12 million people were members of various environmental groups. These are people who realize that, with their voices raised as one, they can have a big say in saving our endangered environment. Eco-groups come in all sizes and flavors. Some are small bands of neighbors fighting against a landfill expansion; other groups have millions of members and are active in passing laws to save forests and wildlife. They all have one thing in common: people joining forces to save our stressed-out planet.

The last 10 years have produced an explosion of environmental groups, all asking for your assistance and money. Sometimes it's tough to decide who to help. In this book we've put together a listing of well-known national groups, what they do best, and what you can expect them to do with your money. (Don't overlook local environmental groups, of which there are too many to mention here. Sometimes the best thing you can do for the environment is join a local group to help clean up your own backyard.)

By joining an eco-group, you add your voice to a growing movement determined to raise awareness of our fragile environment. Following are some of the biggest and most successful eco-groups in the country. But there are many more, especially smaller groups on the local level.

For more information on the kinds of groups you can join, the Public Broadcasting Service (PBS) publishes a book called the Resource Compendium. It lists dozens of organizations and gives suggestions for classroom and community projects.

Write or Call

Resource Compendium, PBS Elementary/Secondary Service, 1320 Braddock Place, Alexandria, VA 22414 (703) 739-5038. Or ask your parents and teachers for the names of local environmental groups in your area you can join. It's fun, and you'll be doing the planet a big favor!

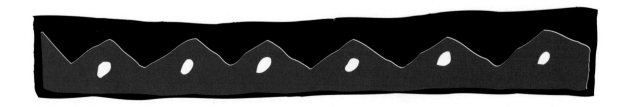

Chapter 2

The Sierra Club

Over 100 years ago, in the spring on 1892, famous naturalist John Muir helped establish the Sierra Club. Formed as a hiking club and wilderness activist group, the Sierra Club was devoted to preserving the beauty of Muir's beloved Sierra Nevada Mountains in California. This included the breathtaking Yosemite Valley, at that time not yet part of Yosemite National Park. Through its work to preserve the Valley, the Sierra Club was at the forefront of the early environmental movement.

The young environmental club supported forest reserves and parks to protect scenic areas from development. They also mapped long-distance trail routes, raised money for trail improvements, and published maps of Yosemite and the Kings River region. They also pioneered mountain climbing routes throughout the Sierras. Mountain climbing is a tradition in the club that endures today.

Today the Sierra Club is one of the largest and most influential environmental groups in the world. It has a multitude of local chapters, and organizes nature treks into the wilderness each year. In addition, the club publishes hundreds of books, films and videos, as well as a monthly magazine, showing people the beauty of the world's pristine wilderness areas. The club's efforts address a wide range of environmental issues, including agriculture, forestry, mining, water, solid waste, urban environment, nuclear energy, renewable energy, wildlife, and others.

John Muir

John Muir, American naturalist and founder of the Sierra Club.

The 600,000-member group believes that the best way to promote conservation of the natural environment is by using our government to pass laws. The Sierra Club puts a lot of effort in convincing public officials to preserve and protect wilderness. It works on hundreds of conservation issues—locally, nationally, and internationally. Most recently the club has worked on the Clean Air Act Reauthorization, Arctic National Wildlife Refuge protection, National Forests and Parks protection, toxic waste laws, global warming and greenhouse effect laws, and many others issues. The group has a lot of muscle when it comes to passing laws, or stopping projects that would hurt the environment. It isn't afraid to take on big governments or companies either.

For example, the Sierra Club has stopped dam construction that would have flooded important wilderness areas. In the 1960s, when two dams were proposed in the Grand Canyon as part of a water works project for Arizona, the club fought against it tooth and nail. They took out an ad in the *New York Times* with the now-famous headline, "Should We Flood the Sistine Chapel So Tourists Can Get Nearer the Ceiling?" Citizen outrage stopped the projects, and increased membership in the club.

More recently, they've fought against legislation in the U.S. Congress that would have opened the Arctic Wildlife Refuge in Alaska to oil exploration. The Club's volunteers work tirelessly to help pass laws cleaning up our air and water. New challenges are also being met head-on, including poor air quality in our cities, toxic-waste dumping, and global warming.

The Sierra Club states its mission this way: "To explore, enjoy and protect the wild places of the Earth; to practice and promote the responsible use of the Earth's ecosystems and resources; to educate and enlist humanity to protect and restore the quality of the natural and human environment; and to use all lawful means to carry out these objectives."

The Sierra Club's legacy of wilderness protection comes from a deep-seated enjoyment of the outdoors. Taking a hike in the woods, the group says, awakens a person's spirit and interest in wilderness preservation. In the words of founder John Muir, "Climb the mountains and get their good tidings."

Membership

$15 Student Rate (includes annual subscription to Sierra magazine)
Send to:
Sierra Club
730 Polk St.
San Francisco, CA 94109

Chapter 3

National Audubon Society

Toward the end of the last century, colorful bird feathers were in style and in great demand for decorating women's hats. Beautiful birds, many of them rare, were slaughtered to get their feathers. Many birds were hunted to near extinction. In 1896, an outraged man by the name of William Brewster began the Massachusetts Audubon Society for the Protection of Birds. The group was named after John J. Audubon, the famous early-American artist and naturalist.

To help stop the slaughter, the group started educating the public about the importance of nature conservation. They also were active in government, helping pass laws protecting birds. In addition, the Society started running wildlife refuges that were off-limits to hunters. Volunteers patrolled the refuges to make sure poachers did not break the law.

Within 10 years Audubon chapters sprouted in several other states and have grown steadily ever since. Today there are over 600,000 members in 500 local chapters, helping pass laws and teaching people the importance of protecting birds and the environment.

At first, members were strictly concerned with wildlife management. In the 1950s and 1960s the insecticide DDT showed how dangerous industrial pollution can be to an entire ecosystem. Birds were dying at an alarming rate when they ate food and insects tainted with DDT. The Audubon Society supported legislation banning DDT and were successful. Many bird species, especially blue birds, have staged a comeback because of the society's efforts.

Today the group is also involved in larger issues like global warming and clean air, as well as wildlife habitat loss. The group's high-priority campaigns focus on ancient forests, wetlands, the Platte River system, and the Arctic National Wildlife Refuge. Audubon fears that if these fragile ecosystems are destroyed, countless birds will be in danger.

Audubon is also actively involved with publishing educational materials, including a newspaper, a birding journal, and *Audubon*, its bi-monthly magazine.

Membership

$20 (includes annual subscription to *Audubon* magazine)
Send to:
National Audubon Society
Membership Data Center
P.O. Box 51000
Boulder, CO 80321-1000

John J. Audubon, American ornithologist and artist.

Chapter 4

The Nature Conservancy

Chaining yourself to a tree doesn't always stop development, and going through the courts or legislature can take years. Some environmental groups believe the solution is simply to buy natural lands to keep the bulldozers away. This keeps the land pristine, protecting sensitive or endangered habitats. After all, the biggest threat to animals facing extinction is loss of habitat, not poaching. (Although poaching, too, takes its toll.)

"To find, protect and maintain the best examples of communities, ecosystems and endangered species in the natural world." That's the mission statement of the Nature Conservancy, an environmental group that uses its donor money to buy land and preserve it from development. The group has over 670,000 members internationally. Purchasing land that species need to survive, the group now owns the largest private system of nature preserves in the world.

The Nature Conservancy owns and manages more than 1,600 private nature preserves across the country. They also help other countries figure out how to set aside lands from development, especially the rainforests of Central and South America.

Nature
Conservancy

*The Nature Conservancy owns and protects many
tracts of land similar to this section of rainforest in Brazil.*

The kinds of lands the Nature Conservancy owns range from small plots -an acre or so (.40 hectare)- near major metropolitan areas, to huge areas of pristine wilderness. Recently, the group bought a 500-square-mile (1,295-square- kilometer) section of New Mexico from a Mexican billionaire after two other environmental groups, the Sierra Club and the Wilderness Society, were unable to get the U.S. government to buy the land and set it aside. Now the land has been set aside and managed in its natural state. No bulldozers allowed.

When you join the Nature Conservancy, you become a member of both the International Nature Conservancy and the local chapter of the state in which you live.

Membership

$25
Send to:
The Nature Conservancy
1815 N. Lynn St.
Arlington, VA 22209

Chapter 5

Greenpeace

Some eco-groups think that the best way to save the environment is through direct action. That means confrontations with those the eco-groups think are hurting the environment. They think that by the time laws are put into effect it will be too late.

One of the best known of these kinds of groups is Greenpeace. They state their mission this way: "Greenpeace is an international organization dedicated to preserving the Earth and all the life it supports. We work to protect the environment from nuclear and toxic pollution, to stop the threat of nuclear power and the production of nuclear weapons and materials, to stop the threat of global warming and ozone layer destruction and to halt the needless slaughter of whales, dolphins, seals and other endangered animals."

Greenpeace is a huge organization, with nearly 2.5 million members in this country alone. Worldwide the figure is around 5 million. The group started over 20 years ago in British Columbia, Canada. A group of people there were against the testing of nuclear bombs on Amchitka Island, one of the Aleutian Islands in Alaska. They managed to find a boat, renamed it *Greenpeace*, and set sail for Alaska to disrupt the test. Said Jim Bohlen, one of the members on the boat, "It was unthinkable that we would not reach our objective, or that it would not matter. Even though [the ship] didn't make it all the way to Amchitka, our tenacity, the dedication of our supporters and an aroused public expressing its outrage resulted in the shutdown of the test site. It is now a wildlife refuge."

Active Greenpeace members believe in "bearing witness," a Quaker tradition of accepting responsibility for being aware of an injustice. Group members bear witness through nonviolent confrontation. They take direct action against what they believe to be atrocities against the environment. In the past, Greenpeace activists used high-speed, inflatable boats to move between protected whales and fishermen's harpoons; they've climbed up smokestacks and hung banners protesting excess air pollution; they've protested nuclear testing in the South Pacific and unsafe nuclear power plants in the United States; they've even chained themselves to railroad tracks leading to a chemical manufacturing plant that makes ozone-depleting CFCs.

Sometimes putting their lives on the line for the safety of the environment ends with tragic results. In 1985 the French government had grown frustrated by Greenpeace's protests against its nuclear tests in the South Pacific. The French Secret Service blew up Greenpeace's ship, the *Rainbow Warrior*, as she lay at harbor. Photographer Fernando Pereira was trapped below deck when the ship submerged, drowning him.

Direct action, though an important part of Greenpeace, is just one of the group's tactics. They also document scientific, financial and political roots of environmental problems, and prepare papers that are presented to courts, the press, and the government. They also publish papers and articles, and produce films and videotapes.

Members of Greenpeace display a protest banner as the aircraft carrier U.S.S. Forrestal crosses under a bridge in New York City.

Greenpeace was the only environmental group not to join in a call to boycott Exxon after the *Valdez* spill in Alaska. Greenpeace said the boycott ignored the real problem...our national dependence on oil. They printed a national ad with a photo of Joseph Hazelwood, captain of the *Valdez*. The headline read, "It wasn't his driving that caused the Alaskan oil spill. It was yours."

Greenpeace has a special membership program just for kids, ages 6 through 12, called P3 (which stands for Earth, the third planet in the solar system). P3 members get a regular newsletter detailing important issues facing the environment. In a recent issue, the danger to the Earth's ozone hole was explained. Readers were told what steps they could take to help, like cutting back on CFCs, the chemical in refrigerators and air conditioners that eats up the ozone layer.

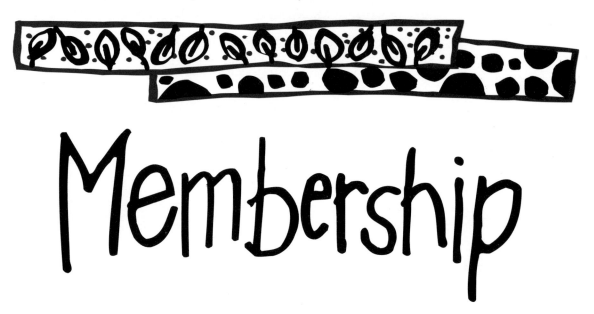

Membership

$12
Send to:
Greenpeace/P3 Team
1436 U Street, NW
Washington, D.C. 20009

Chapter 6

National Geographic

Although not an "eco" group in the strictest sense, the National Geographic Society has its roots in a broad understanding of the world and its environment. If we don't know our geography, how can we possibly understand the environmental crisis in the world? Gilbert M. Grosvenor, president of the Society, says, "Without geographic knowledge, citizens cannot possibly understand that an ozone hole over Antarctica affects people in New York, or that the destruction of tropical forests in Brazil influences the climate of Chicago."

The sad fact is that most Americans do not understand geography. In a recent survey, one in seven Americans couldn't even find the United States on a map. One in four couldn't find the Pacific Ocean, even though it covers a third of the Earth's surface. A study of 12th graders found that "most students did not demonstrate an understanding of the basic concepts of physical and cultural geography." More than 20 percent thought incorrectly that removing vegetation from an area would increase wildlife population. Many thought the greenhouse effect was caused by an increase of solar flares on the sun.

To truly comprehend global environmental problems, like the destruction of the rainforest, kids need to learn about geography. It's not just about dull maps and charts. It's a way of looking at the Earth to see how everything is connected to each other. The National Geographic Society has launched a huge effort to teach geography in our schools and through books, magazines and videos that the Society produces. By joining the Society, you support efforts like these that make people aware of how destroying an ecosystem in one part of the world truly effects all of us. Plus you get a great magazine that's been published since 1888 as well.

Membership

$21 (includes 12-month subscription to *National Geographic Magazine*)
Send to:
National Geographic Society
P.O. Box 2895
Washington, D.C. 20077-9960

Chapter 7

Kids for Saving Earth

Clinton Hill was a sixth-grader in New Hope, Minnesota, when he started a club called Kids for Saving Earth (KSE). Clinton knew that if kids did even small things...conserving water at home, recycling, car pooling or biking...they could make a big difference in helping the environment. Sadly, Clinton died of cancer shortly after KSE was formed. But his parents and friends, wanting to carry on his dream, started looking for ways to make KSE grow.

In 1989, Target Stores, a division of Dayton Hudson Corporation, got involved. With Target's help, KSE became an international group, with 21,000 club chapters and 630,000 members worldwide in 45 countries. Club members emphasize helping nature by conserving and cleaning up right in their own backyards. They involve family members by working with them to conserve at home. They also do things like march in parades to inspire community members to protect the Earth.

Kids for Saving Earth memberships are free, and include certificates, educational materials and a quarterly mailing of KSE News. Each club is encouraged to choose what works best for its members. KSE knows that there are no single answers to our environmental problems. It's up to the kids to get creative and find hands-on solutions.

Kids for Saving Earth has members all over the world who help clean up the environment right in their own backyards.

For example, the KSE Club in Vladivostok, Russia, started their group to raise environmental awareness and to inform their neighborhood about the Earth. They regularly take field trips to nearby forests and lakes to help gather glass, bottles and old cans that litter the landscape. In Zimbabwe, Africa, the KSE Club knows that tree planting will help preserve the earth. So, besides learning and teaching the community about conservation, they are active in planting many trees to help stop soil erosion. In El Monte, California, the Twin Lakes Elementary School KSE Club started its own recycling business. They sell items that are made by recycling materials, and the money is used to adopt endangered animals. So far, they've adopted three manatees and one humpback whale.

Membership

Membership is free. To get more information about joining a KSE Club, or about starting your own group, stop at any Target Store to pick up member registration material and a newsletter. Most stores have info at a "KSE Information Station" near the snack bar. If there's no Target store near you, write:

Kids for Saving Earth, P.O. Box 47247, Plymouth, MN 55447-0247.

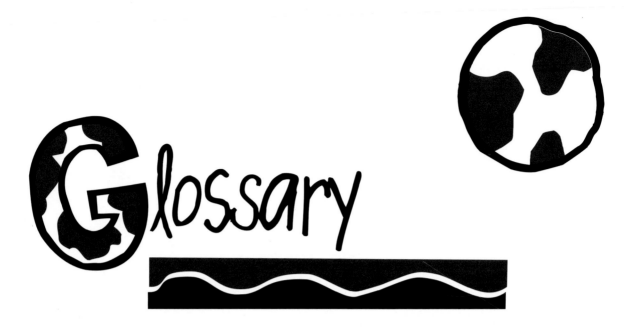

Glossary

CFCs

Gasses made up of carbon, hydrogen, chlorine, and fluorine. CFCs were once widely used in aerosol sprays and refrigerants. Now because of fears of what CFCs do to the ozone layer (see *Ozone*), CFCs are gradually being phased out.

Conservation

The controlled use and protection of Earth's natural resources, like forests and rivers.

DDT

An insecticide used widely during the 1940s and 1950s to kill insect pests. Though it helped increase crop yields, scientists discovered that DDT remained in the environment for many years, spreading through the ecosystem as larger animals and fish ate enough tainted insects to reach toxic levels. DDT is very poisonous to humans; eating lots of fish or birds tainted with the insecticide can be very dangerous. Because of these discoveries, DDT was banned by the government in the 1970s. Unfortunately, small amounts of DDT can be found in fish and birds even today. It is a chemical that is very difficult to get rid of. Such concerns have led to governmental regulation and the replacement of toxic insecticides that persist in the environment (like DDT) by compounds that break down more quickly into nontoxic forms.

Ecosystem

A community of plants and animals in an environment supplying the raw materials for life, i.e., chemical elements (or food) and water. An ecosystem is defined by climate, altitude, latitude, water, and soil characteristics, and other physical conditions. When pollution enters an ecosystem, the whole balance of life can be thrown out of balance, resulting in plant and animal deaths or extinction.

Endangered

A species of plant or animal is said to be endangered if its ability to survive is seriously in question. Usually, species are placed on endangered lists because of the activities of humans. Some ways species can become endangered are: unrestricted hunting or loss of habitat; use of toxic pesticides, oil spills, strip mining, water pollution, draining of wetlands, cutting down of forests, etc.

Erosion

The way in which the Earth's surface is constantly worn away, usually because of running water, waves, glaciers or wind. The erosion of farmland topsoil is a big problem, especially in the United States. Ways to combat erosion include reforestation, terracing, and special plowing techniques.

Extinction

When a plant or animal species is completely wiped out, never to be seen again. (See *Endangered*.)

Forestry

The management of forest resources, such as wood, water, wildlife and recreation.

Global warming
(See *Greenhouse effect*.)

Greenhouse effect
The Earth is surrounded by a layer of invisible gasses (the atmosphere). When the sun's rays shine down, much of the heat is trapped by these gasses, acting much like the glass in a greenhouse. This is good, because we need heat to survive. However, since we started burning fossil fuels in our factories and homes (coal, oil, gas, etc.), new amounts of gasses have been entering the atmosphere, like carbon dioxide. Many scientists believe these extra gasses will heat up the Earth even more. An increase in atmospheric carbon dioxide of 10% over the past century makes some scientists predict a long-term warming of our climate.

Naturalist
One who knows a lot about natural history, especially zoology or botany.

Ozone
Ozone is the most chemically active form of oxygen. It has a fresh, penetrating odor, and can often be smelled right after a thunderstorm. Most ozone is formed in the ozone layer of the atmosphere. The ozone layer keeps some of the sun's rays, which can be harmful to life, from reaching the Earth's surface. Scientists fear that some pollutants, like CFCs, are thinning the ozone layer, which could mean more of the sun's ultraviolet rays will reach us, causing damage to animals and plants alike.

Poacher
A person who hunts or fishes illegally on the property of somebody else.

Recycling

Instead of automatically throwing everything we consume out with the garbage (and having our landfills steadily run out of room), many people today recycle their materials, thereby putting less demand on factories to use up our raw natural resources. The recycling of noncombustible products such as glass and metals (like aluminum cans) is growing and offers long-range hope for our solid waste disposal problems.

Renewable energy

Unlike coal or oil, which is used up when it's burned (and pollutes the atmosphere), renewable energy sources are always there, waiting to be tapped. Renewable energy sources include the energy from water and wind; geothermal energy, the Earth's internal heat that is released naturally in geysers and volcanoes; tidal energy, the power released by the ebb and flow of the ocean's tides; and solar energy. Unfortunately, in order to use these forms of energy, big advances in technology must first be made to make them more economical than coal or oil.

Toxic waste

Toxic wastes are often made in factories as a byproduct, and include heavy metals (like mercury, lead, and cadmium), certain hydrocarbons, and other poisons. Such substances are usually sealed in metal drums and deposited underground or in the ocean, but the containers often corrode and leak, polluting the land and water supply.

Wildlife refuge

When a plant or animal becomes endangered (*see endangered*), one way to protect them is to set aside land for their exclusive use. Usually, the biggest danger to wildlife isn't poaching or pollution, it's loss of habitat (through construction or mining, etc.) Such destruction can endanger the lives and breeding grounds of a large number of species simultaneously. In recent years environmentalists have pressed for the establishment of new wildlife refuges and for land-use planning.

References

Berle, Peter A. A. "The Naure of Audubon." *Audubon*, November-December, 1991, p.6(1).

"A Centenial Celebration: 1892-1992." *Sierra*, May-June, 1992, p.52(22).

Cook, James. "The World is Our Theme." *Forbes*, January 21, 1991, p.42(4).

"Defending the Earth" *Scholastic Update*, April 19, 1991, p.27(1).

Gifford, Bill. "Inside the Environmental Groups." *Outside*, September 1990, p. 69(13).

Grosvenor, Gilbert M. "Grasping Nature Through Geography." *Business Week*, June 18, 1990, p.S13(1).

Horton, Tom. "The Green Giant." *Rolling Stone*, Sept. 5, 1991, p. 42(9).

Lavine, Carolyn S. "The Nature Conservancy Turns 40." *Conservationist*, July-August, 1990, p.24(5).

"Nature's Avengers." *Scholastic Update*, April 19, 1991, p.20(2).

Scott, Geoff. "Grouping Together to Protect the Environment." *Current Health*, January 2, 1992, p.28(2).

Starr, Deborah. "Adopt-An-Acre." *Horticulture*, December, 1990, p. 18(2).

Index

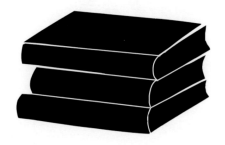

TARGET EARTH™ COMMITMENT

At Target, we're committed to the environment. We show this commitment not only through our own internal efforts but also through the programs we sponsor in the communities where we do business.

Our commitment to children and the environment began when we became the Founding International Sponsor for Kids for Saving Earth, a non-profit environmental organization for kids. We helped launch the program in 1989 and supported its growth to three-quarters of a million club members in just three years.

Our commitment to children's environmental education led to the development of an environmental curriculum called Target Earth™, aimed at getting kids involved in their education and in their world.

In addition, we worked with Abdo & Daughters Publishing to develop the Target Earth™ Earthmobile, an environmental science library on wheels that can be used in libraries, or rolled from classroom to classroom.

Target believes that the children are our future and the future of our planet. Through education, they will save the world!

TARGET®

Minneapolis-based Target Stores is an upscale discount department store chain of 517 stores in 33 states coast-to-coast, and is the largest division of Dayton Hudson Corporation, one of the nation's leading retailers.